The
Mysterious
Ms. Martin

Jeanie Stewart
Illustrated by Ilene Richard

A Harcourt Achieve Imprint

www.Rigby.com
1-800-531-5015

Literacy by Design Leveled Readers: *The Mysterious Ms. Martin*

ISBN-13: 978-1-4189-3792-8
ISBN-10: 1-4189-3792-4

Printed in China
3 4 5 6 7 8 985 14 13 12 11 10 09 08

Contents

1

Maple Mysteries

All the way home from the library, I had trouble keeping up with my cousin Lan. She is only a year older than I, yet her legs are longer, and she always seems to be in a hurry. I begged her to slow down, but she was anxious to get home and start reading the Maple Kids Mystery she had just checked out. We are both big fans of the Maple Kids Mystery books.

I don't know why, but Lan had checked out *The Maple Kids' Mall Mystery* again, even though she'd already read it twice. She has, actually, read *every* book in the series twice. We'd seen a poster at the bookstore saying that the next book in the series—*The Maple Kids' Vacation Mystery*—would be out soon. Every day since then, we'd gone to the library looking for it, but they still didn't have it.

I started up the front steps of our house and then remembered that the lock on our front door was broken. Before I could turn around, however, the door opened, and Grandma stepped outside with Ms. Martin, our next-door neighbor.

"Ms. Martin knows all about locks, so she fixed our door," Grandma told us cheerfully.

Ms. Martin smiled and tucked a tiny screwdriver into her pocket. "In my work, a person learns about all sorts of things," she told us as she headed back toward her house.

Grandma believed that Ms. Martin could do anything because lately Ms. Martin had been helping her learn how to write in English. "Ms. Martin is so nice to help me, and she brought a surprise for you children, too."

Grandma pointed to a book on the table, and my heart leaped with joy

when I read its cover: *The Maple Kids' Vacation Mystery* by J.A. Jones! Although I wanted to read it first, I let Lan take it. After all, she was starting the series for the third time, and I still had *The Maple Kids' Stolen Car Mystery* to read. She got comfortable on the sofa by the window, and I settled into my favorite reading place, the big chair by the lamp. I was just getting to an exciting part when Lan interrupted me.

"I wonder where this book came from, Hao," she said.

I held my finger on the sentence I was reading so that I wouldn't lose my place and reminded her that it came from Ms. Martin.

"I know, but if the book store and the library couldn't get this book yet, how did Ms. Martin get a copy?" Lan asked, and she pressed her finger against her lips, just the way Mindy Maple does when she thinks about a mystery.

2

Lan
the Detective

Lan likes to pretend that she is a great detective like Mindy Maple. She's always looking for a mystery to solve, yet every time she finds one, things never go quite the way she plans. Plus she wants me to be Mason Maple, her trusty helper, and she is always getting me caught up in her wild ideas.

I held my book in front of my face, trying to ignore her, but Lan wouldn't give up.

Lan informed me that she noticed right away that our new book wasn't in a bookstore bag. I patiently suggested that maybe Grandma took the book out

of the bag before giving it to us. Lan didn't like that explanation, and she wrinkled her forehead the way Mindy Maple does when she's thinking about clues. "I also noticed that there is no price sticker on this book, Hao."

Sighing, I reminded Lan that the book was a gift and that people don't usually leave price tags on gifts. She hesitantly admitted that was true, yet she added, "But if there were a price sticker on this book, it would have left a sticky spot." She rubbed her fingers across the book cover to show me that there wasn't a sticky spot anywhere, saying, "Hao, I think Ms. Martin stole this book!"

I said that maybe Ms. Martin worked in a bookstore and could get books early, but Lan just shook her head.

"I don't think she works anywhere because she never leaves her house except to go to the post office or the supermarket," Lan said, looking out the window toward Ms. Martin's house.

When I asked Lan how she knew that, Lan blushed and let the curtain fall back into place. She's always getting into trouble for being nosey. She claimed that she had just happened to notice. But I warned her that she was doing it again: imagining a mystery, just so she could pretend to be Mindy Maple. She looked shocked and protested that she would never do that.

"What about the mystery of Mr. Va?" I asked.

Last winter, right after Lan read *The Maple Kids' Spy Mystery,* she decided that our neighbor Mr. Va was a spy. For a week she uncovered clues and made up ideas about him, but, of course, she had been wrong.

Offended, she pointed out that Mr. Va was always sitting in his backyard at night, just looking around. "You have to admit that having a telescope on his back porch was very odd."

"It's not odd for someone who likes to study the stars!" I begged Lan to forget the mystery of Ms. Martin and let me read my book, but I had hardly finished a page before she interrupted me again.

"OK, maybe I've been wrong before, but this time is different. I just *know* there is a mystery about Ms. Martin!"

15

3

Backyard Spies

After dinner Grandma went to her room to work on her writing lesson while Lan and I did the dishes. Lan, however, was more interested in talking about Ms. Martin than she was in getting the dishes clean.

"Have you ever noticed how much mail Ms. Martin gets?" she asked, handing me a plate that still had food stuck to it.

"No, did you notice this plate was still dirty?" I replied, handing the plate back to her.

Lan wiped the plate again while talking about how strange it was that Ms. Martin knew how to fix a lock. She was really starting to bug me, so I suggested that maybe Ms. Martin's job was fixing locks that people mailed to her.

"Be serious, Mason!" Lan responded and then covered her mouth guiltily with her hand.

"You called me Mason!" I shouted, waving the dishtowel at her. "That's proof that you're pretending to be Mindy."

I reminded her for the thousandth time that we weren't Mason and Mindy and that there wasn't any mystery in our real lives.

She insisted that mysteries happen in real life, too, reminding me that last year our neighbor Mr. Yuri's car got stolen. She was so busy talking about the car theft that she handed me a pan without rinsing it at all.

"Remember, Hao, Ms. Martin got a new car around that *very same time*," she concluded with a Mindy Maple look on her face.

I didn't bother pointing out that Mr. Yuri's car had been green, yet Ms. Martin's new car was blue.

"We have to investigate," Lan decided, not noticing that she was drying her hands on my shirt. I didn't really want to study Ms. Martin's behavior, but I also thought I should try to keep Lan out of trouble.

Moments later we were hiding behind the fence that separates Ms. Martin's backyard from ours, peering at her back door. We didn't have to wait long, surprisingly, for seconds later Ms. Martin exited the house dressed entirely in black: black pants, black shoes, black shirt. Lan raised her eyebrows at me as Ms. Martin pulled on black gloves.

I suggested she might be cold. But Lan pointed out that it was April, so she couldn't be *that* cold. And when Ms. Martin pulled a black ski mask over her head, even *I* had to admit that it looked odd.

21

"Just as I thought. . . . Ms. Martin is a cat burglar!" Lan hissed, ducking behind a rose bush.

"Why would Ms. Martin want to steal cats?" I joked.

Lan pulled me down beside her and explained that cat burglars don't steal cats: they steal treasure from people's houses. They're just called cat burglars because they dress in black, sneak around, and climb like cats.

By now I was laughing, so she said angrily, "I know you read *The Maple Kids' Cat Burglar Mystery,* Hao. So quit pretending you don't know what I'm talking about!"

I explained that I had only been joking, but Lan didn't find it funny. Instead, she ordered me to check on Ms. Martin's movements.

I stood on tiptoe and peered over the fence, but I didn't see Ms. Martin anywhere. Forgetting we were supposed to be hiding, Lan jumped up and cried, "Oh, no! We let her get away!"

Lan was preparing to search the whole, entire neighborhood when suddenly Ms. Martin's face popped up on the other side of the fence—right in front of us!

4

Police Visit

Lan jumped back, landing on my foot, and we both shrieked. (While Lan had yelled out in fear, I had yelled out in pain—she almost broke my foot!) Then Ms. Martin pulled off the mask and gloves. "Based on your screams, I conclude that you weren't able to see me when I was in the shadows. Am I right?"

"Y-y-yes," I muttered, my voice croaking like a frog's. Ms. Martin seemed satisfied, and before Lan or I could say another word, she dashed back into her house.

"That was very strange," I remarked, rubbing my sore foot. "Maybe we should tell Grandma."

Lan didn't like that idea one bit, and I knew why. Grandma would be angry to hear that Lan was being nosey again. I agreed not to tell, but I still wanted to go back inside. Lan, however, peeked over the fence again and announced that we couldn't go yet because she had just heard a car come to a stop in front of Ms. Martin's house. "Let's get closer so we can see who it is!"

25

We dashed to the front yard and saw a police officer at the door, talking to Ms. Martin as his car sat in front of the house. From our hiding place behind the bushes we heard him say something about a robbery case and ask Ms. Martin if she would be home tomorrow. She said she was going out early, but she would be home all afternoon.

"OK, then I'll be back tomorrow with the fingerprinting tools," the officer said, waving good-bye and leaving.

Lan gasped and whispered that she had been right that Ms. Martin was a robber, adding, "Why else would that police officer want to fingerprint her?"

Lan carefully started planning to follow Ms. Martin when she left her house tomorrow morning. I sighed, for I knew I'd be going along. Someone had to be there to keep reminding Lan that she was *not* Mindy Maple.

5

Museum Puzzle

The very next morning, we followed Ms. Martin to the art museum. When I stopped to look at a beautiful painting of a castle, Lan yanked on my sleeve so hard that I nearly fell over. She was only interested in looking at Ms. Martin, not the paintings.

I told her to stop rushing me, adding, "You are not Mindy Maple, and there is no mystery here: Ms. Martin is just looking at art."

Lan pulled me behind a statue and asked, "Then why is she writing in that notebook?"

I explained that Ms. Martin was probably taking notes about her favorite paintings, just like a lot of people do.

Lan responded that Ms. Martin wasn't even looking at the paintings. I peeked around the statue and saw that Ms. Martin was staring at the ceiling.

"I believe she is checking out the burglar alarm and video cameras," Lan said in her Mindy Maple voice.

"Where are the cameras? Do you think we're being filmed right now?" I asked, combing my hair with my fingers to make sure it looked neat.

Lan gave me the sort of look Mindy Maple gives Mason when he is not being very smart. Then she said that we needed to find out what Ms. Martin was writing.

Her pencil moving quickly across the page, Ms. Martin seemed to be drawing something. Suddenly she stopped, ripped the page from her notebook, crushed it into a ball, and quickly threw it into the trash can.

As soon as Ms. Martin disappeared around the corner, Lan rescued the ball of paper and smoothed it out. Studying it carefully, she put one hand against her forehead the way Mindy Maple does when she makes an important discovery.

"Maybe you'll believe me now, Hao, for this is a diagram of this room."

When I didn't look impressed, she waved the paper in my face and yelled, "Don't you get it? Ms. Martin is an art thief, and she's going to rob the museum!"

6
Grandma Disagrees

"**B**ut Grandma, if you want us to, we can prove that Ms. Martin is an art thief. We have evidence!"

Grandma stared at Lan as if she were confused. Thinking Grandma didn't understand the meaning of *evidence,* I explained that *evidence* meant "proof." Grandma said she knew that, but she *didn't* understand why we thought our nice neighbor would rob a museum.

Lan handed the wrinkled paper to Grandma and told

her that Ms. Martin had drawn a map
of the museum so that she'd know where
the burglar alarms and cameras were.
Grandma said that was silly and that
Ms. Martin wasn't a robber. Unconvinced,
Lan asked Grandma to tell her what
Ms. Martin *did* do, then.

"She writes. . . . Don't you see how
nicely she writes?" Grandma replied,
picking up her notebook and turning
to a page Ms. Martin had written
while helping Grandma with her
English lessons.

I agreed that it was very nice writing, but Lan hardly even looked at it and whispered to me, "You shouldn't think that a thief can't have pretty handwriting!"

Overhearing Lan, Grandma frowned and gave us a serious talk in Vietnamese about being nice, having respect for adults, and minding our own business. To make sure we'd learned our lesson, she stacked some of her famous banana muffins on a plate and told us to take them next door to Ms. Martin.

Lan tried to protest, but Grandma shook her head and warned us not to mention any more foolishness, adding, "And don't forget to thank Ms. Martin for fixing our lock and for giving you the wonderful book."

Grandma Disagrees

35

As we stood on Ms. Martin's porch, Lan reached for the doorbell, but I stopped her and said, "Maybe Ms. Martin isn't home, and we can just set the muffins on the porch and leave."

"Shhh . . . I *know* she's home because I can hear her talking to someone."

The window next to the front door was open, so Lan peeked through it and motioned for me to join her. Ms. Martin was talking on the phone, and although I didn't want to listen, her voice rang loudly through the window screen.

"I think a bank robbery would be too challenging, so I've decided to go with the art robbery instead."

Lan's eyes widened and she hissed, "I was right!"

I wanted to run home, but Lan refused, certain that Grandma wouldn't believe us without more evidence. Before I could stop her, she rang the doorbell.

7

Finding Proof!

Smiling at us, Ms. Martin said that she was just coming over to our house to tell Grandma that she couldn't help her with her English lessons tomorrow, adding, "I have some important work that I must finish."

Lan pushed me forward, and I held the plate of muffins toward Ms. Martin, speechless. While Lan quickly explained that Grandma had sent us over to thank Ms. Martin for being such a good neighbor, I just stood there.

Pleased, Ms. Martin held the door open and invited us inside to share the muffins. All I wanted to do was run home. But Lan blocked my path, and I had no choice but to follow Ms. Martin into the house.

My hands shook as I set the muffins on the table. Ms. Martin was getting some milk from the refrigerator when the phone rang. She asked us to excuse her, explaining that she was expecting an important phone call.

The minute Ms. Martin left the room, Lan started searching through a stack of letters on the table to look for evidence, commenting, "See, I told you she gets a lot of mail."

I warned Lan to stop being so nosey, but she just said, "This isn't even her mail. . . . It's addressed to J.A. Jones. I think she steals mail, too, Hao!"

"That name sounds very familiar," I said, scratching my head the way Mason Maple does when he's puzzled. Not really listening to me, Lan remarked

that Jones is a very common name and continued to hunt for evidence.

Suddenly the door opened, and Ms. Martin stepped into the room, saying into her cordless phone, "Why, yes, I *do* have a couple of nosey detectives in my kitchen."

Lan dropped the envelopes she was holding, and I reached for a chair because my knees felt like rubber bands. Ms. Martin lowered her voice and added, "I think they have figured out the mystery of what I do for a living."

8

Getting
the Facts

Grandma was on the phone, checking up on us! Smiling, Ms. Martin handed the phone to Lan and began to pour us glasses of milk. I picked up the mail Lan had dropped and stacked it neatly on the counter. Seeing the name J.A. Jones on the envelopes suddenly reminded me where I'd seen the name before.

"J.A. Jones is the author of the Maple Kids Mysteries!" I exclaimed, turning around and staring at Ms. Martin. "You *are* a writer!"

Ms. Martin laughed and admitted that she was the author of our favorite mystery series, explaining that writers sometimes use other names. J.A. Jones was the name she used when she wrote for children.

When Lan finished talking to Grandma, she joined us at the table. Blushing with embarassment, she explained, "Grandma told us you were a writer, but we thought she meant you had good handwriting."

Ms. Martin didn't seem upset at all. She said that she actually enjoyed Lan's active imagination, and that Lan reminded her of herself when she was a young girl. "When I saw you two in the art museum today, I knew you were on the trail of another mystery."

I couldn't believe that Ms. Martin had seen us! While I felt guilty for following her, Lan (still being nosey) asked why Ms. Martin had created the drawing of the museum.

"As I was telling my editor on the phone earlier, I've decided that my next book will be about an art robbery— *The Maple Kids' Art Museum Mystery.* I drew that diagram so I could remember exactly the way the room was arranged. I always check the settings of my books to make sure they are true to life. My first diagram got a bit messy, so I threw it out and started a new one."

I asked if she'd been checking book facts when we saw her sneaking around in dark clothing last night. She explained that she was testing to see if a person could really hide in the shadows by wearing dark clothing at night. Then Lan asked why the police officer had visited her.

"Officer Abello is a friend of mine. He's the one who taught me about locks, and he's coming here soon to teach me about fingerprinting so that I can get all the facts right in my next book. Would you like to stay and learn about fingerprints?"

Lan shouted, "Yes!" and began bouncing up and down in her chair, just the way Mindy Maple does when she gets excited. I told her to calm down, reminding her once again that she *wasn't* Mindy Maple.

"Well, actually she is," Ms. Martin laughed. "Or maybe I should say that Mindy Maple is Lan. You see, I modeled my two favorite characters after my two favorite neighbors."

"You mean *we're* Mindy and Mason?" I asked, excited.

Ms. Martin nodded, and Lan shouted, "I get it—*Maple* is Mindy and Mason's last name because we live on Maple Street!" She brushed her hair back behind her ears and crossed her arms just the way Mindy Maple does when she solves a mystery. "See, Hao," she bragged, "I *told* you there was a mystery next door!"